PIANO/VOCAL/GUITAR

JUSTIN TIMBERLAKE
THE 20/20
EXPERIENCE

ISBN 978-1-4803-4503-4

HAL•LEONARD® CORPORATION

7777 W. BLUEMOUND RD. P.O. BOX 13819 MILWAUKEE, WI 53213

For all works contained herein:
Unauthorized copying, arranging, adapting, recording, Internet posting,
public performance, or other distribution of the printed music in this publication is an infringement of copyright.
Infringers are liable under the law.

Visit Hal Leonard Online at
www.halleonard.com

PUSHER LOVE GIRL

Words and Music by JUSTIN TIMBERLAKE,
JAMES FAUNTLEROY, JEROME HARMON,
TIM MOSLEY and CHRIS GODBEY

Moderately slow

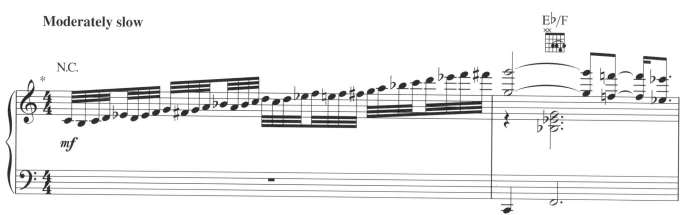

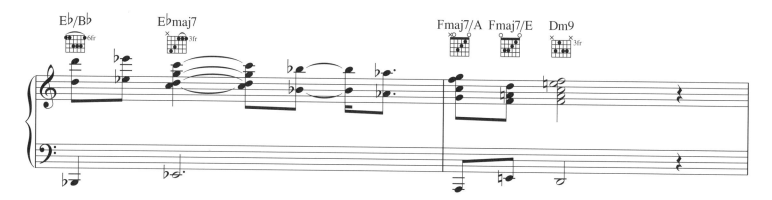

Recorded a half step lower.

Copyright © 2013 by Universal Music - Z Tunes LLC, Tennman Tunes, Almo Music Corp., Underdog West Songs, Fauntleroy Music, Warner-Tamerlane Publishing Corp.,
Jerome Harmon Productions, WB Music Corp., Virginia Beach Music and B Max Entertainment Publishing
All Rights for Tennman Tunes Administered by Universal Music - Z Tunes LLC
All Rights for Underdog West Songs and Fauntleroy Music Controlled and Administered by Almo Music Corp.
All Rights for Jerome Harmon Productions Administered by Warner-Tamerlane Publishing Corp.
All Rights for Virginia Beach Music Administered by WB Music Corp.
International Copyright Secured All Rights Reserved

Hey, lit-tle ma-ma, ain't got-ta ask me if I want to. Just tell me, can I

get a light? Roll you up and let it run through my veins. __ 'Cause

I can al-ways __ see the far-thest stars __ when I'm on you.

'cause all I want is you, _____ babe, _____ yeah. _____ One more time.
(Roll me up _____ a lit-tle with you, _____ ba - by.) _____

So high I'm on the ceil-ing, ba - by. So go on and be my deal-er, ba - by,
(Push - er love.) (Be my drug.)

'cause all I want is you, _____ ba - by, _____ one more time.
(Hook me up _____ a lit - tle with you _____ ba - by.) _____

SUIT & TIE

Words and Music by JUSTIN TIMBERLAKE, JAMES FAUNTLEROY,
SHAWN CARTER, JEROME HARMON, TERRANCE STUBBS,
JOHNNY WILSON, CHARLES STILL and TIM MOSLEY

Copyright © 2013 by Universal Music - Z Tunes LLC, Tennman Tunes, Almo Music Corp., Underdog West Songs, Fauntleroy Music, WB Music Corp.,
Carter Boys Music, Warner-Tamerlane Publishing Corp., Jerome Harmon Productions, Dynatone Publishing Company and VB Rising Publishing
All Rights for Tennman Tunes Administered by Universal Music - Z Tunes LLC
All Rights for Underdog West Songs and Fauntleroy Music Controlled and Administered by Almo Music Corp.
All Rights for Carter Boys Music Administered by WB Music Corp.
All Rights for Jerome Harmon Productions Administered by Warner-Tamerlane Publishing Corp.
All Rights for Dynatone Publishing Company Administered by Unichappell Music Inc.
All Rights for VB Rising Publishing Administered by ole
International Copyright Secured   All Rights Reserved
-contains a sample of "Sho Nuff" by Terrance Stubbs, Johnny Wilson and Charles Still, © 1974 (Renewed) Dynatone Publishing Company

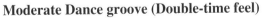

Moderate Dance groove (Double-time feel)

___ go-in' out so hot, just ___ like an ov-en. And I'll _____ burn ___ my - self, but just ___ had to

Dmaj7

touch it. But, it's ___ so fire _____ and it's ___ all mine. ___ Hey, ___ ba - by,

Em7

we don't mind ___ all the watch-in'. Hah, _____ 'cause

if they stud - y close, real close, they might ___ learn some-thin'. She ___ ain't

noth-in' but a lit-tle doo-zy when __ she does it. She's __ so fire _____ to - night.

And __ as long as I got my suit and tie, __ I'm-a leave it all on the floor to-night. __

And you got fixed up to the nines. __ Let me show you a few things (show you a few things).

All pressed up in black and white __ and you dressed in that dress I like. __

at it. Ooh, __ so thick, now I know why they call __ it a fat-ty. And aww, __

sh*t so sick, got a hit and picked __ up a hab-it. That's __ al - right, _____ 'cause you're __ all

mine. __ And aww, _____ go on and show 'em who you __ call dad - dy. I guess

they're just mad __ 'cause, girl, they wish __ they had it. Ooh, my kill-er, my thrill - er, yeah, __ you're a

D.S. al Coda

clas - sic and you're _ all mine _____ to - night.

CODA

Get out your seat, Hov.

Half-time feel

Rap: *(See additional lyrics)*

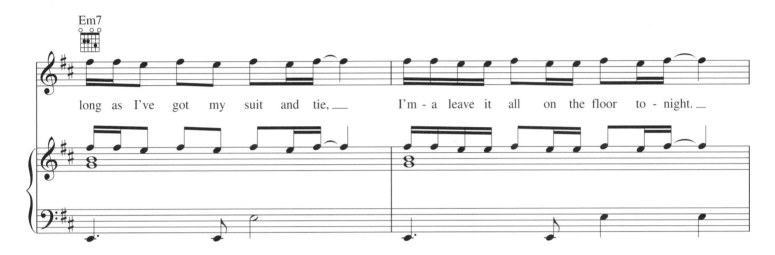

long as I've got my suit and tie, __ I'm - a leave it all on the floor to - night. __

And you got fixed up to the nines. __ Let me show you a few things (show you a few things).

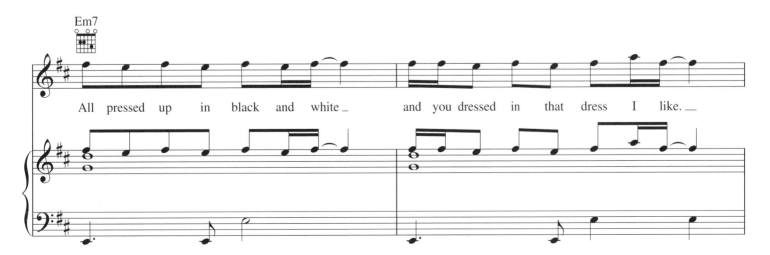

All pressed up in black and white __ and you dressed in that dress I like. __

Da, da, da, nah._____ *Vocal ad lib.*

Additional Lyrics

Rap: All black at the white shows. White shoes at the black shows. Green card for the Cuban linx.
Y'all sit back and enjoy the light show. Nothin' exceeds like excess. Stoute got gout from havin' the best of the best.
Is this what it's all about? I'm at the restaurant, my rant disturbin' the guests. Years of distress, tears on the dress.
Tryin' to hide her face with some make-up sex. Uhh, this is truffle season. Tom Ford tuxedos for no reason.
AllSaints for my angel. Alexander Wang, too. Ass-tight denim and some Dunks. I'll show you how to do this young!
Uhh, no papers, catch vapors. Get high, out Vegas. D'usses on doubles, ain't lookin' for trouble.
You just got good genes so a nigga try'n a cuff you. Tell your mother that I love her 'cause I love you.
Tell your father we go farther as a couple. They ain't lose a daughter, got a son. I show you how to do this, hon'.

DON'T HOLD THE WALL

Words and Music by JUSTIN TIMBERLAKE,
JAMES FAUNTLEOY, JEROME HARMON,
TIM MOSLEY and CHRIS GODBEY

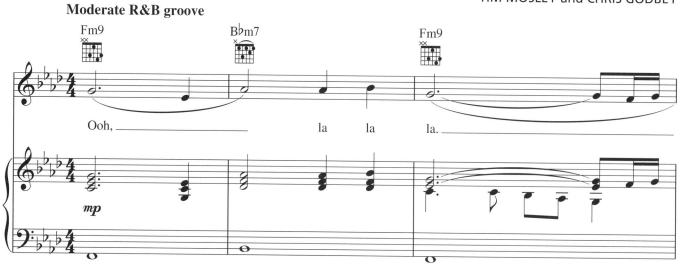

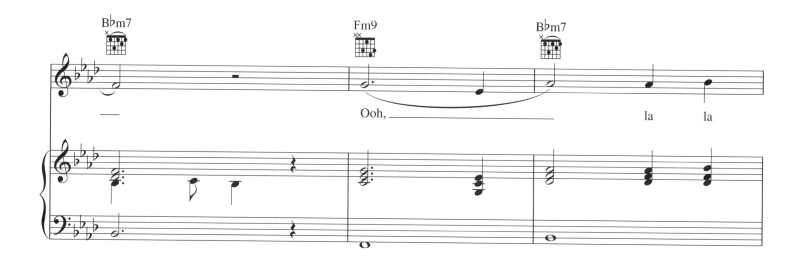

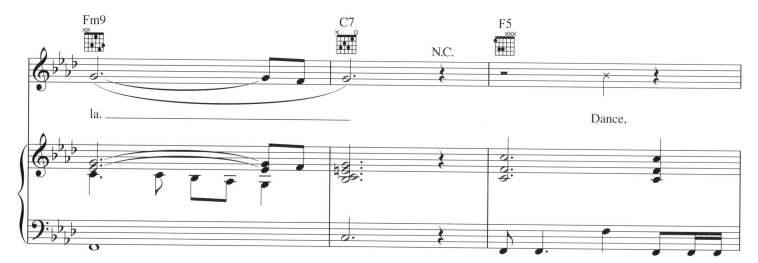

Copyright © 2013 by Universal Music - Z Tunes LLC, Tennman Tunes, Almo Music Corp., Underdog West Songs, Fauntleroy Music, Warner-Tamerlane Publishing Corp.,
Jerome Harmon Productions, WB Music Corp., Virginia Beach Music and B Max Entertainment Publishing
All Rights for Tennman Tunes Administered by Universal Music - Z Tunes LLC
All Rights for Underdog West Songs and Fauntleroy Music Controlled and Administered by Almo Music Corp.
All Rights for Jerome Harmon Productions Administered by Warner-Tamerlane Publishing Corp.
All Rights for Virginia Beach Music Administered by WB Music Corp.
International Copyright Secured All Rights Reserved

don't hold the wall.   Dance,   don't, don't, don't hold the wall.

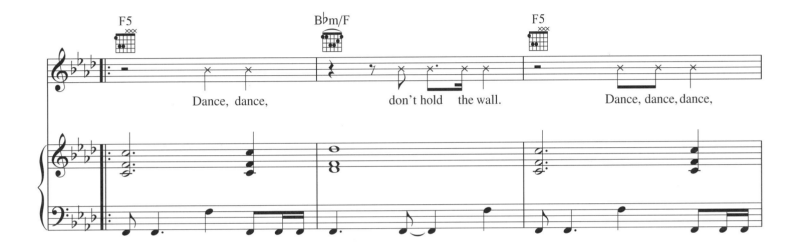

Dance, dance,   don't hold the wall.   Dance, dance, dance,

don't hold the wall.   Come on ___ the floor ___ with them legs,
                        I think ___ I heard ___ what you said,

it's get - ting down ___ but I'll get up.   'Cause I heard ___ you tell ___ your   girl -
he's not ___ what you thought and you're fed up.   I heard ___ your girl - friend tell ___

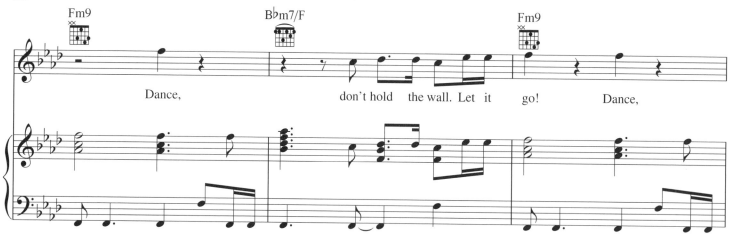

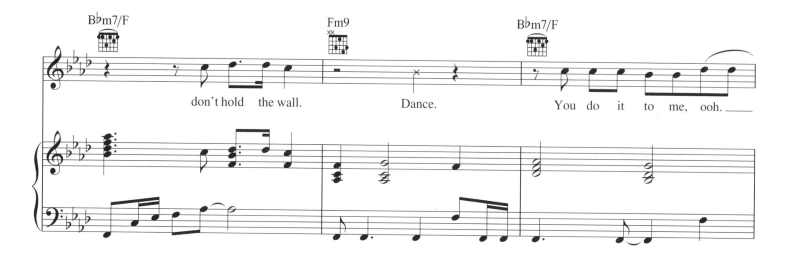

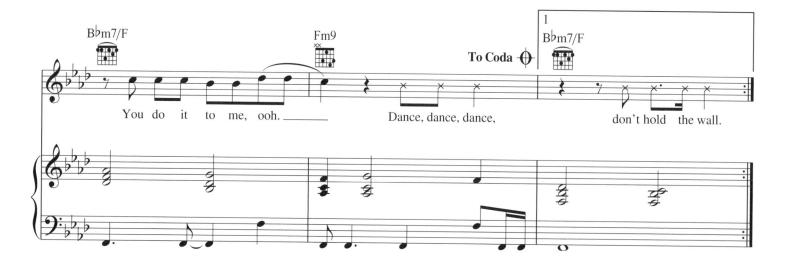

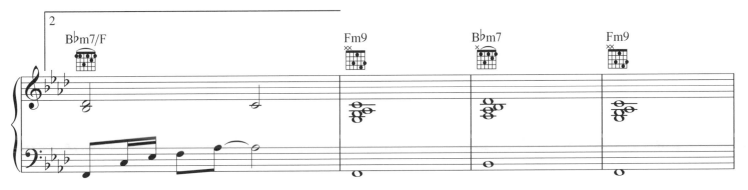

Dance, don't hold the wall.

Dance, don't hold the wall.

Ba - by, hold up.

CODA

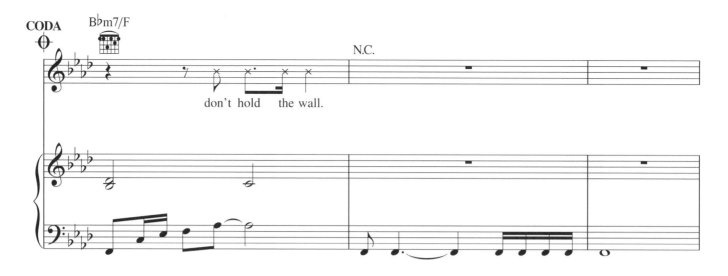

don't hold the wall.

R.H. tacet 1st time

Well? How do you like it? You

should-n't have to ask me that ques - tion.   Well?   Al - right.

How do you like   it?   I

love   it,   love   it.   Al - right.

Come on ___ the floor ___ with them legs,   it's get - ting down ___ but I'll get up.

Well? Come on and dance,
Dance,

come on, ba - by, next to ___ me. ___ Take ___ my

hand, get on the floor, ___ come on, ba - by, dance with ___ me. ___

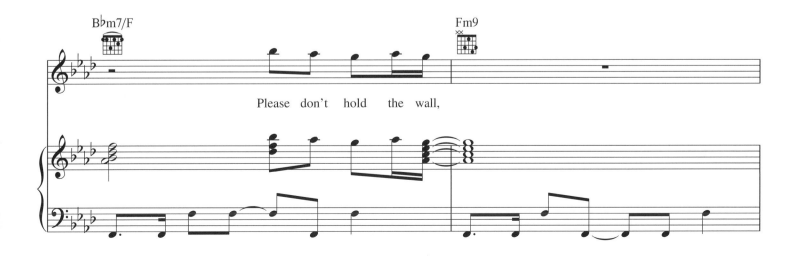

Please don't hold the wall,

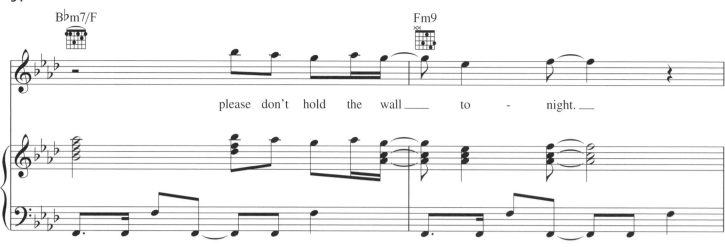

please don't hold the wall ___ to - night. ___

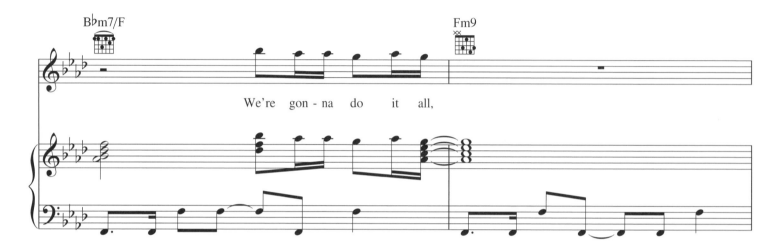

We're gon - na do it all,

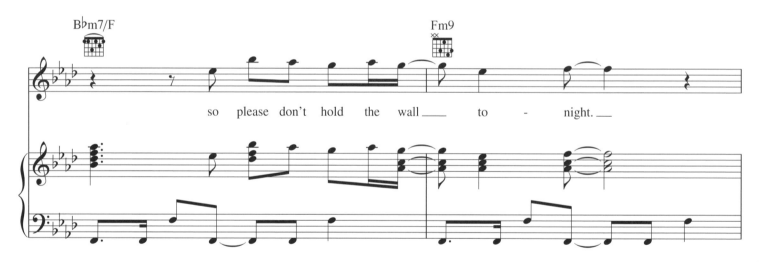

so please don't hold the wall ___ to - night. ___

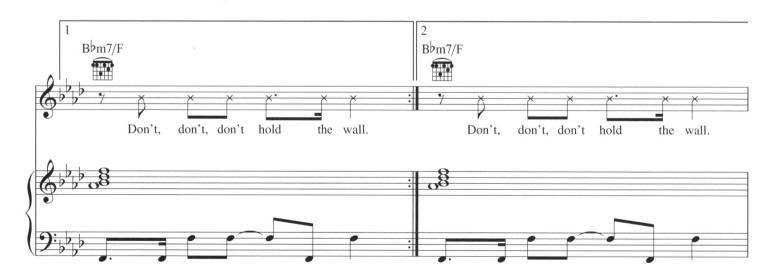

Don't, don't, don't hold the wall.   Don't, don't, don't hold the wall.

Dance,

don't, don't, don't hold the wall.

Dance,

don't hold the wall.　　Dance,　　don't hold the wall.

STRAWBERRY BUBBLEGUM

Words and Music by JUSTIN TIMBERLAKE,
JAMES FAUNTLEROY, JEROME HARMON,
TIM MOSLEY, CHRIS GODBEY
and GARLAND MOSLEY

Moderate Funk groove

Copyright © 2013 by Universal Music - Z Tunes LLC, Tennman Tunes, Almo Music Corp., Underdog West Songs, Fauntleroy Music, Warner-Tamerlane Publishing Corp.,
Jerome Harmon Productions, WB Music Corp., Virginia Beach Music, B Max Entertainment Publishing and 757 Music
All Rights for Tennman Tunes Administered by Universal Music - Z Tunes LLC
All Rights for Underdog West Songs and Fauntleroy Music Controlled and Administered by Almo Music Corp.
All Rights for Jerome Harmon Productions Administered by Warner-Tamerlane Publishing Corp.
All Rights for Virginia Beach Music Administered by WB Music Corp.
International Copyright Secured   All Rights Reserved

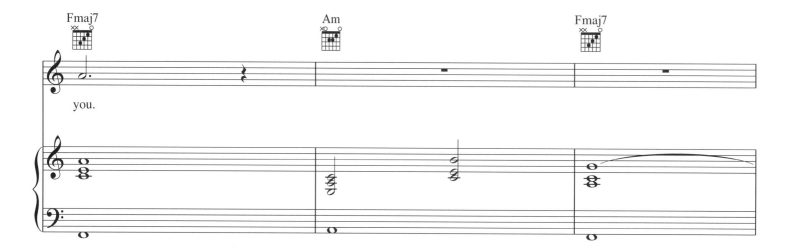

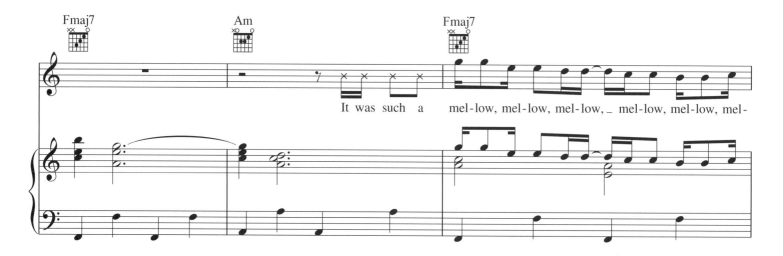

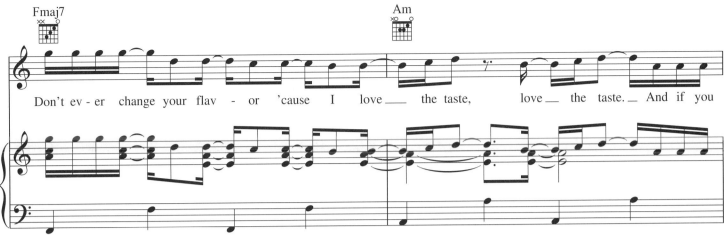

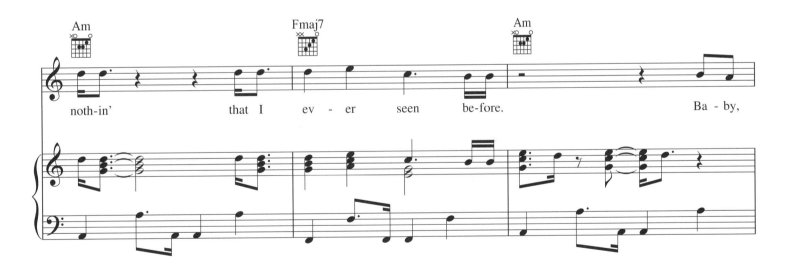

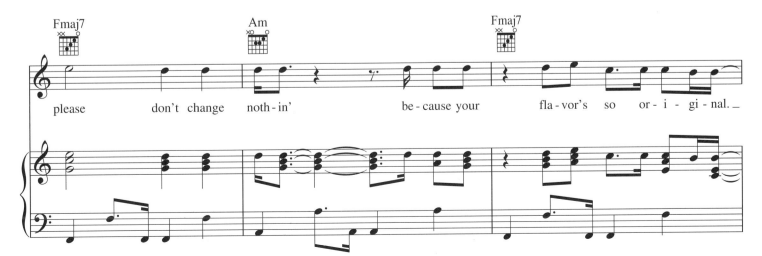

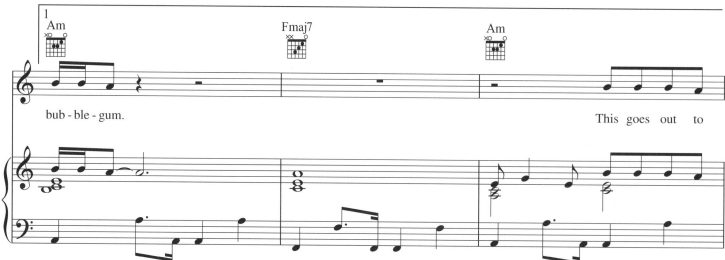

you, you, you, you, you, yeah.

This goes out to you, you, you, yeah. So tell me

2

bub - ble - gum. My lit - tle straw - ber - ry, straw - ber - ry, straw - ber - ry

bub - ble - gum. My lit - tle straw - ber - ry, straw - ber - ry, straw - ber - ry

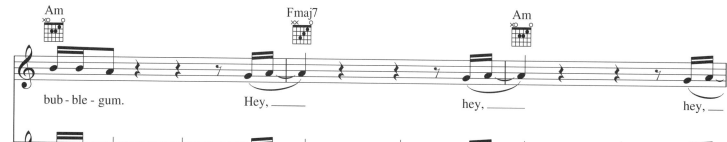

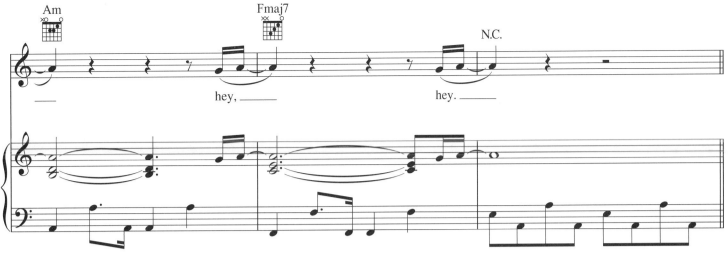

Double-time Samba feel

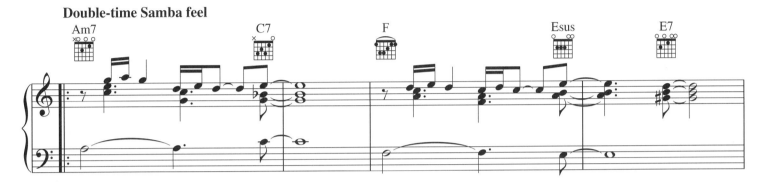

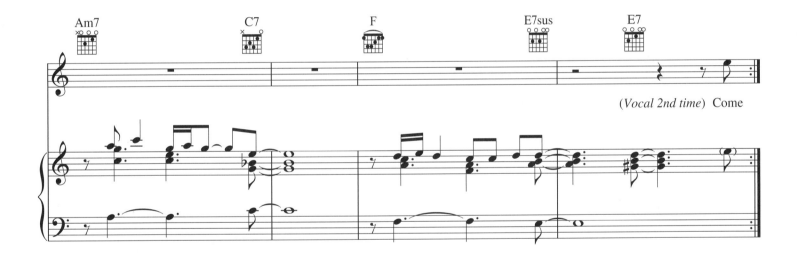

(*Vocal 2nd time*) Come

in,   sit down. ___ Let me el - e - vate ___ your ap - pe - tite, ___   an -

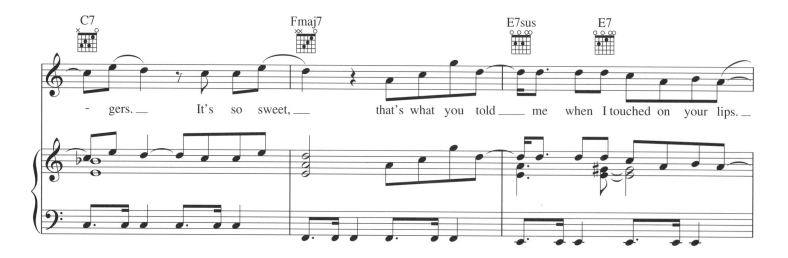

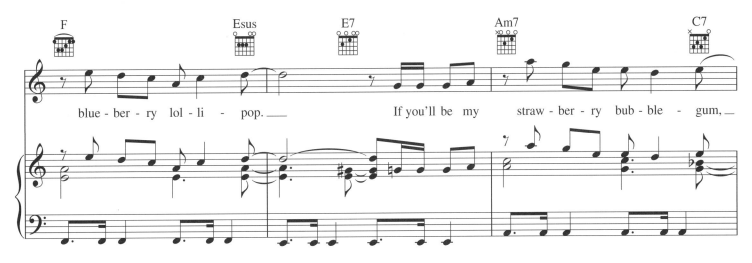

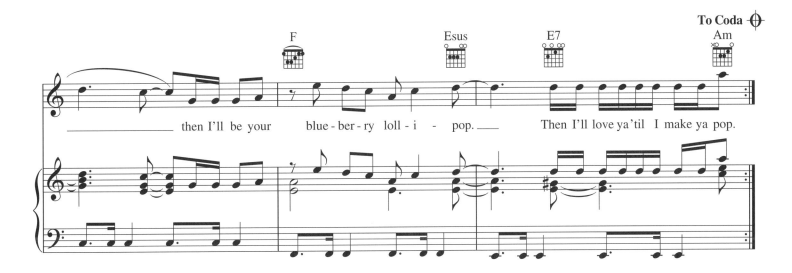

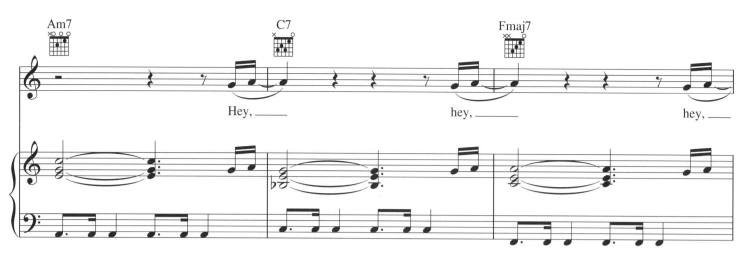

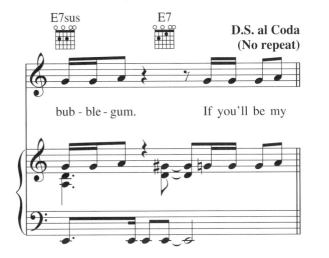

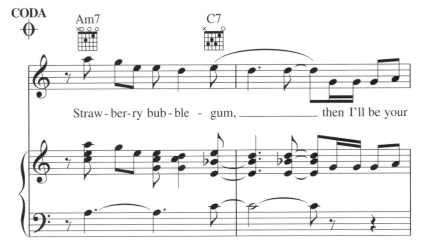

TUNNEL VISION

Words and Music by JUSTIN TIMBERLAKE,
JAMES FAUNTLEROY, JEROME HARMON,
TIM MOSLEY, CHRIS GODBEY
and GARLAND MOSLEY

Moderately fast Hip-Hop

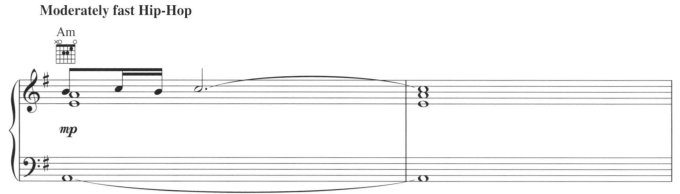

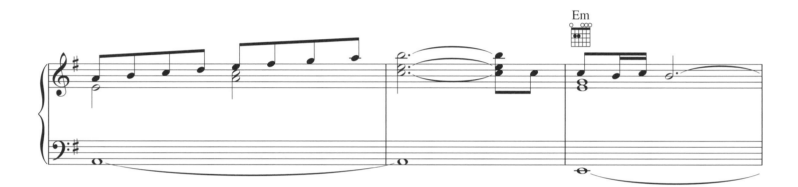

Copyright © 2013 by Universal Music - Z Tunes LLC, Tennman Tunes, Almo Music Corp., Underdog West Songs, Fauntleroy Music, Warner-Tamerlane Publishing Corp.,
Jerome Harmon Productions, WB Music Corp., Virginia Beach Music, B Max Entertainment Publishing and 757 Music
All Rights for Tennman Tunes Administered by Universal Music - Z Tunes LLC
All Rights for Underdog West Songs and Fauntleroy Music Controlled and Administered by Almo Music Corp.
All Rights for Jerome Harmon Productions Administered by Warner-Tamerlane Publishing Corp.
All Rights for Virginia Beach Music Administered by WB Music Corp.
International Copyright Secured   All Rights Reserved

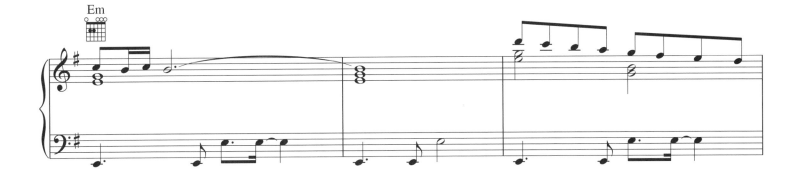

Don't know why, _ but girl   I'm feel - in' close _ to   you,   may - be it's this o - cean view.
Now that I   know _ the truth,   what _ am I s'posed _ to do?

I'm so e - mo - tion - al and   all these thoughts come danc - in' on my head
Chang - in' up ___ and break - in' all my rules ___ ev - er since we   met.

for too long, ___ too long, ___ too long. ___
I'm so gone, ___ I'm so gone, ___ I'm so gone. ___

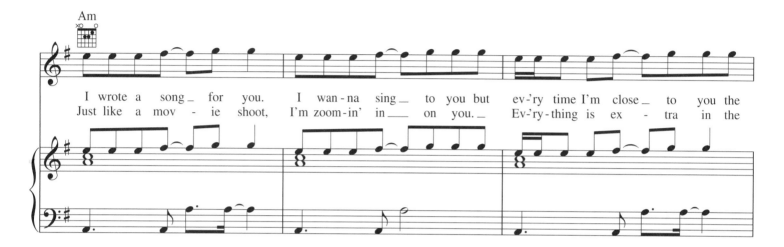

Am

I wrote a song ___ for you. I wan-na sing ___ to you but ev-'ry time I'm close ___ to you the
Just like a mov-ie shoot, I'm zoom-in' in ___ on you. ___ Ev-'ry-thing is ex-tra in the

Em

words wan-na come out but I for-get. It's so strong, ___
back-ground, just fades in-to the set as we ride ___

Am

___ it's so strong, ___ it's so strong. ___ It ___ might ___
___ off ___ in-to the sun. ___

seem ____ like ____ I'm ____ catch - ing some - thing, that's be - cause it's

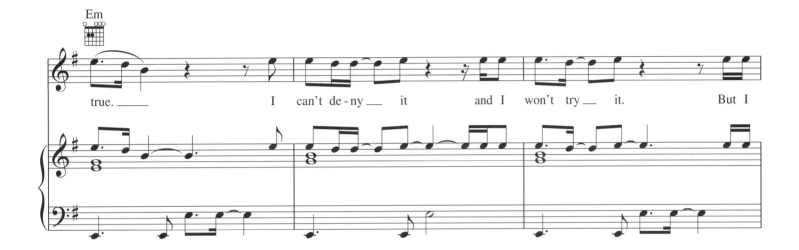

true. ____ I can't de - ny ___ it and I won't try ___ it. But I

think that ___ you ___ know. I _____ look a - round, and ev - ry -

thing I see is beau - ti - ful 'cause all I see is you. And I

can't de - ny __ it and I stand by __ it. And I won't hide it an - y - more.

A crowd - ed room an - y - where, a mil - lion peo - ple a - round all I see is

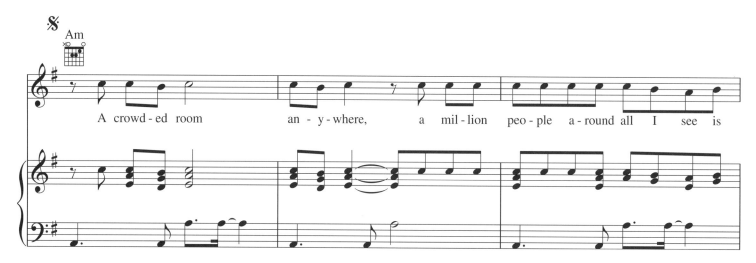

you there. Ev - 'ry - thing just dis - ap - pears, dis - ap - pears,

dis - ap - pears, __ dis - ap - pears, yeah. A mil - lion peo - ple in a

crowd-ed room but my cam - 'ra lens-es on - ly get set____ to zoom and it all be -

comes so clear, be - comes so clear, be - comes so clear.____

I got that tun-nel vis - ion for you.____ I got that

tun-nel vis - ion for you.____ I got, I got that tun-nel vis - ion for you.____

Lyrics:
—— you, —— yeah. —— Zoom, zoom, zoom, zoom, zoom, zoom,

zoom, zoom, zoom, zoom, zoom, zoom, zoom in on you. In,

in, in, in on you, I on-ly see —— you, —— yeah. —

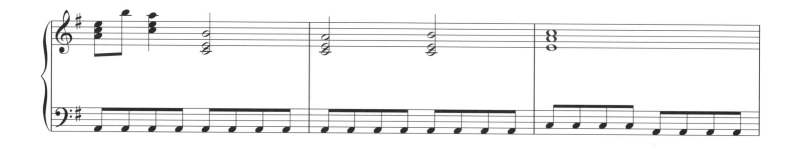

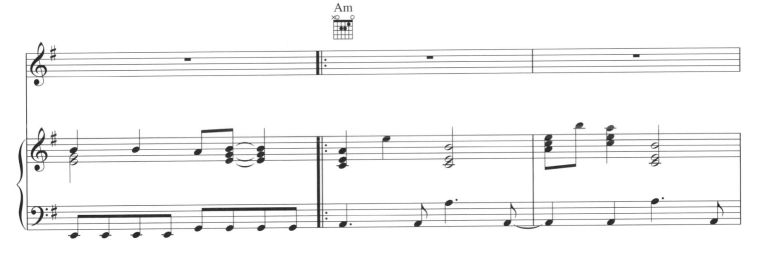

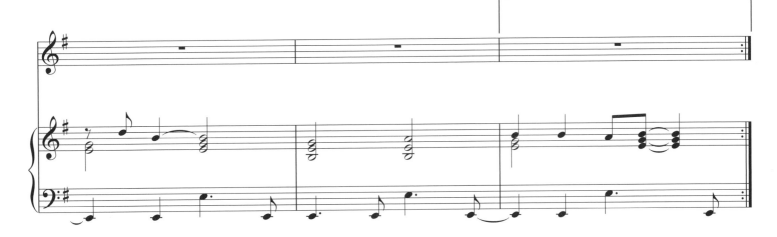

D.S. al Coda

CODA

tun - nel vis - ion, I on - ly see ___

you, ___ yeah. ___

I on-ly see ___ you, ___ yeah. ___

I on-ly see ___ you, ___ yeah. ___

SPACESHIP COUPE

Words and Music by JUSTIN TIMBERLAKE,
JAMES FAUNTLEROY, JEROME HARMON,
TIM MOSLEY, CHRIS GODBEY
and GARLAND MOSLEY

Copyright © 2013 by Universal Music - Z Tunes LLC, Tennman Tunes, Almo Music Corp., Underdog West Songs, Fauntleroy Music,
Warner-Tamerlane Publishing Corp., Jerome Harmon Productions, WB Music Corp., Virginia Beach Music, B Max Entertainment Publishing and 757 Music
All Rights for Tennman Tunes Administered by Universal Music - Z Tunes LLC
All Rights for Underdog West Songs and Fauntleroy Music Controlled and Administered by Almo Music Corp.
All Rights for Jerome Harmon Productions Administered by Warner-Tamerlane Publishing Corp.
All Rights for Virginia Beach Music Administered by WB Music Corp.
International Copyright Secured   All Rights Reserved

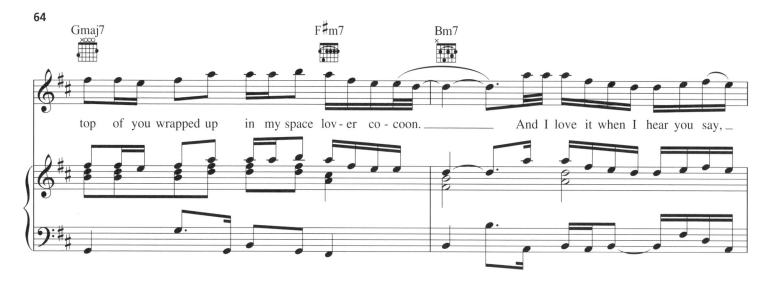

top of you wrapped up in my space lov-er co-coon. _____ And I love it when I hear you say, _

ooh, ooh, ooh, ooh, ooh, ooh, ooh, ooh, ooh, ooh. Sing to me. I love it when I hear you say, _

ooh, ooh, ooh, ooh, ooh, ooh, ooh, ooh, ooh, ooh. Sing to me. Now,

Sing to me, sing to me. Now break it down. Babe, ___ this is the part, _

this is the part _____ where you and me _____ and all of the stars _____

col - lide ___ to - night. This is the part, ___ (this is the part) ___ where we take ___

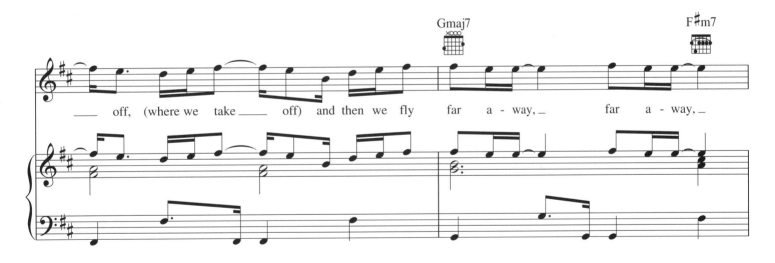

___ off, (where we take ___ off) and then we fly far a - way, ___ far a - way, ___

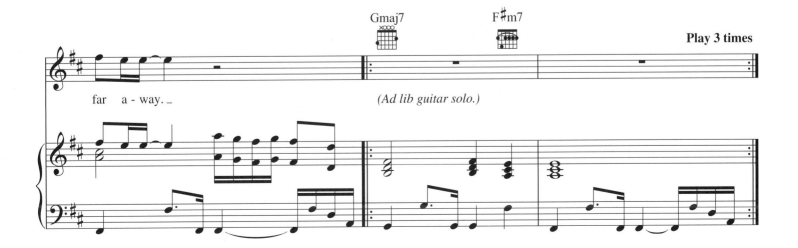

Play 3 times

far a - way. ___   *(Ad lib guitar solo.)*

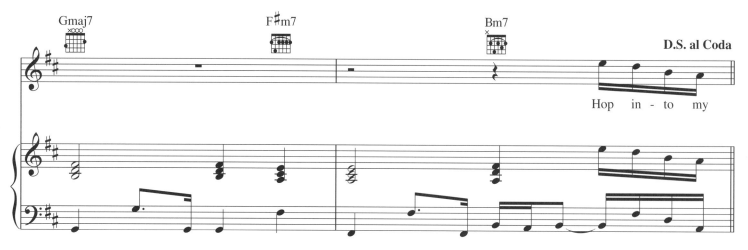

D.S. al Coda

Hop in - to my

top of you wrapped up in my space lov - er co - coon._____

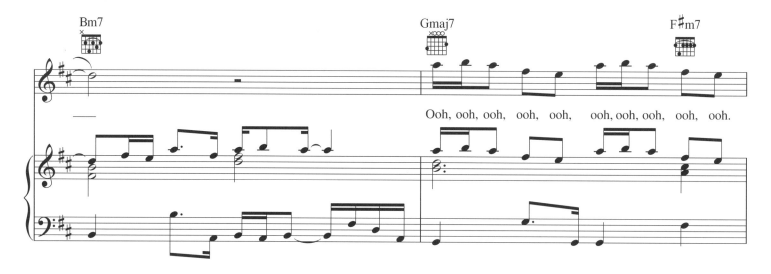

Ooh, ooh, ooh, ooh, ooh, ooh, ooh, ooh, ooh, ooh.

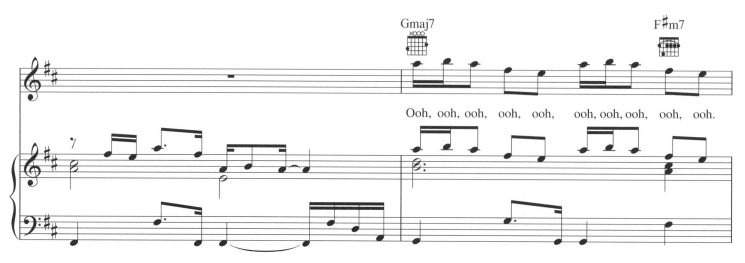

Ooh, ooh, ooh, ooh, ooh, ooh, ooh, ooh, ooh, ooh.

Ooh, ooh, ooh, ooh, ooh, ooh, ooh, ooh, ooh, ooh.

Ooh, ooh, ooh, ooh, ooh, ooh, ooh, ooh, ooh, ooh.

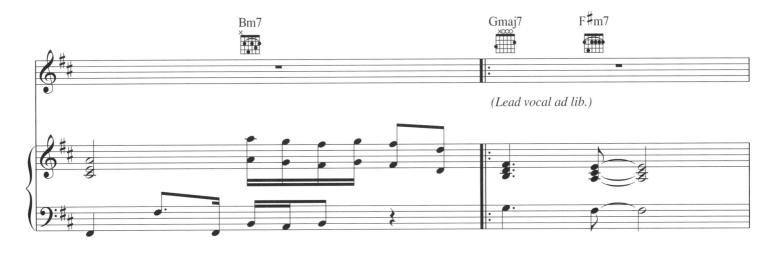

(Lead vocal ad lib.)

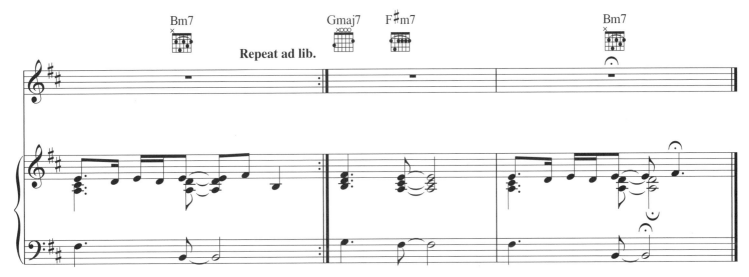

Repeat ad lib.

THAT GIRL

Words and Music by JUSTIN TIMBERLAKE,
JAMES FAUNTLEROY, JEROME HARMON,
TIM MOSLEY, CHRIS GODBEY
and NOEL WILLIAMS

Slow R&B groove

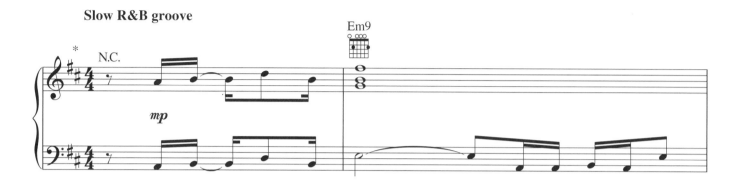

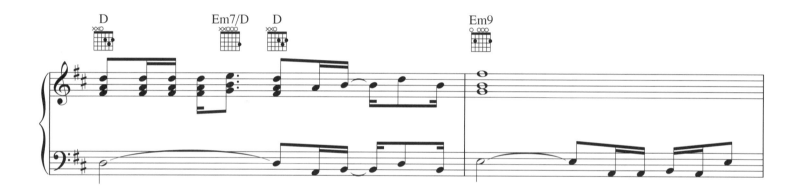

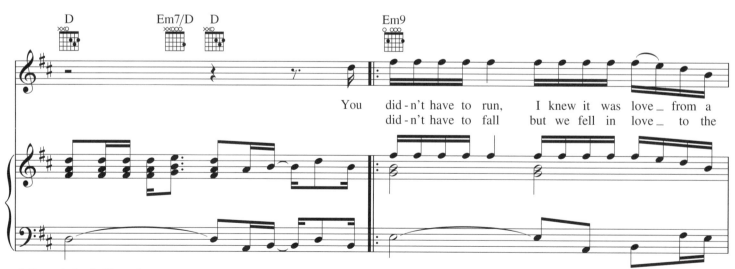

You did-n't have to run, I knew it was love_ from a
did-n't have to fall but we fell in love_ to the

Recorded a half step lower.

Copyright © 2013 by Universal Music - Z Tunes LLC, Tennman Tunes, Almo Music Corp., Underdog West Songs, Fauntleroy Music, Warner-Tamerlane Publishing Corp.,
Jerome Harmon Productions, WB Music Corp., Virginia Beach Music, B Max Entertainment Publishing, Calderwood Inc. and Haka Taka Music
All Rights for Tennman Tunes Administered by Universal Music - Z Tunes LLC
All Rights for Underdog West Songs and Fauntleroy Music Controlled and Administered by Almo Music Corp.
All Rights for Jerome Harmon Productions Administered by Warner-Tamerlane Publishing Corp.
All Rights for Virginia Beach Music Administered by WB Music Corp.
International Copyright Secured   All Rights Reserved

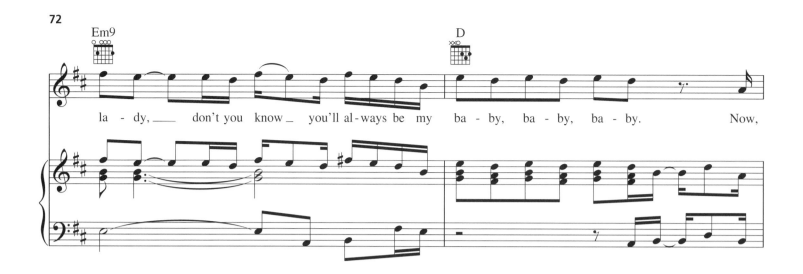

la - dy, ___ don't you know ___ you'll al - ways be my ba - by, ba - by, ba - by. Now,

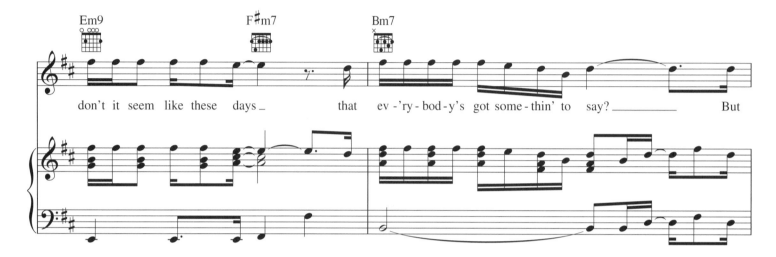

don't it seem like these days ___ that ev-'ry-bod-y's got some-thin' to say? _____ But

I _____ don't pay at - ten - tion to the talk, ba - by. _____ And,

I don't real - ly care ___ if they stop and stare 'cause they'll see my num - ber

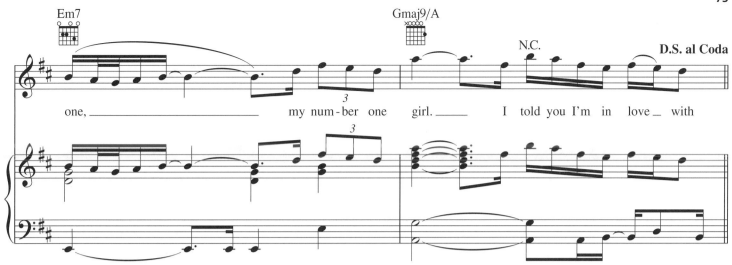

one, _____ my num-ber one girl. _____ I told you I'm in love _ with

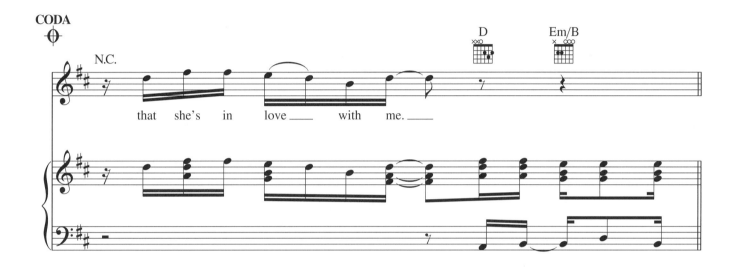

CODA

that she's in love ____ with me. ____

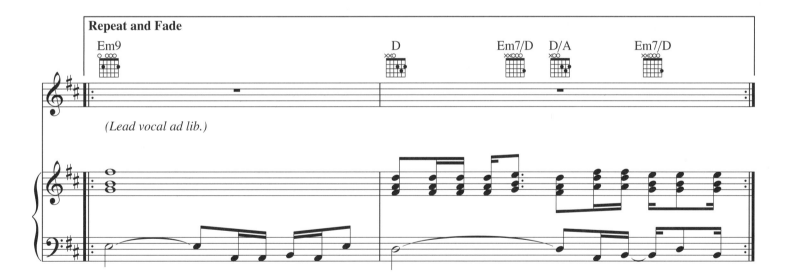

Repeat and Fade

(Lead vocal ad lib.)

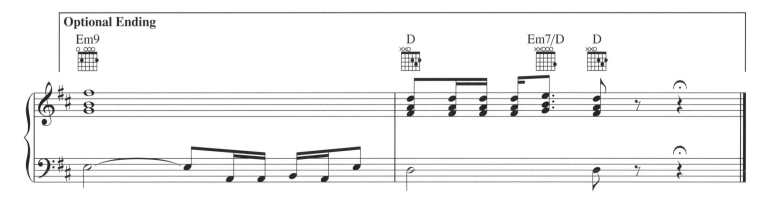

Optional Ending

LET THE GROOVE GET IN

Words and Music by JUSTIN TIMBERLAKE,
James Fauntleroy, Jerome Harmon,
Tim Mosley and Chris Godbey

Syncopated groove

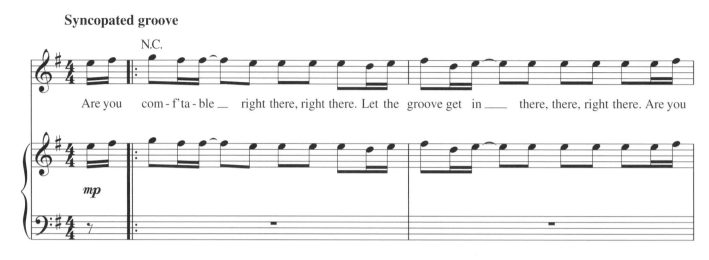

Are you com-f'ta-ble __ right there, right there. Let the groove get in __ there, there, right there. Are you

com-f'ta-ble __ right there, right there. Let the groove get in __ there, there, right there. Are you

com-f'ta-ble __ right there, right there. Let the groove get in __ there, there, right there. Are you

Copyright © 2013 by Universal Music - Z Tunes LLC, Tennman Tunes, Almo Music Corp., Underdog West Songs, Fauntleroy Music, Warner-Tamerlane Publishing Corp.,
Jerome Harmon Productions, WB Music Corp., Virginia Beach Music and B Max Entertainment Publishing
All Rights for Tennman Tunes Administered by Universal Music - Z Tunes LLC
All Rights for Underdog West Songs and Fauntleroy Music Controlled and Administered by Almo Music Corp.
All Rights for Jerome Harmon Productions Administered by Warner-Tamerlane Publishing Corp.
All Rights for Virginia Beach Music Administered by WB Music Corp.
International Copyright Secured   All Rights Reserved

know you got some-thing to prove.__ Ba-by, Ma-ma, move,__ like the
know you got noth-ing to lose.__ Make it move,__ girl you

groove's tak-ing o-ver you.__ Make no mis - take, you're in the
know what we came to do.__

place to be __ by far.__ So let's get cra - zy like we ain't

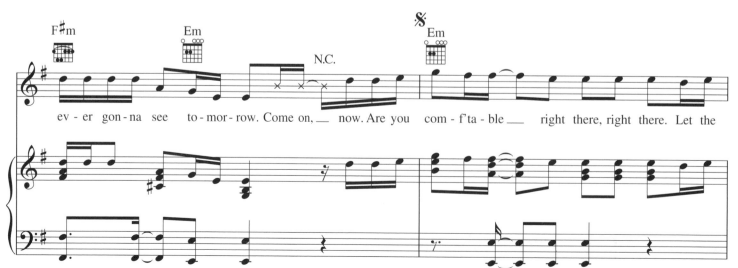

ev - er gon-na see to-mor-row. Come on,__ now. Are you com-f'ta-ble __ right there, right there. Let the

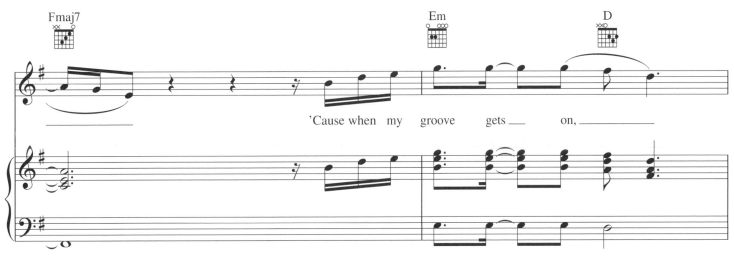

'Cause when my groove gets ___ on, ___

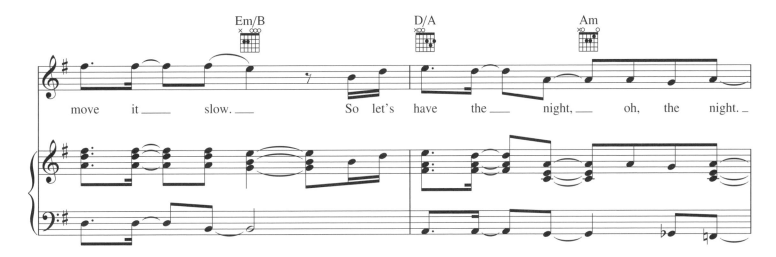

move it ___ slow. ___ So let's have the ___ night, ___ oh, the night. ___

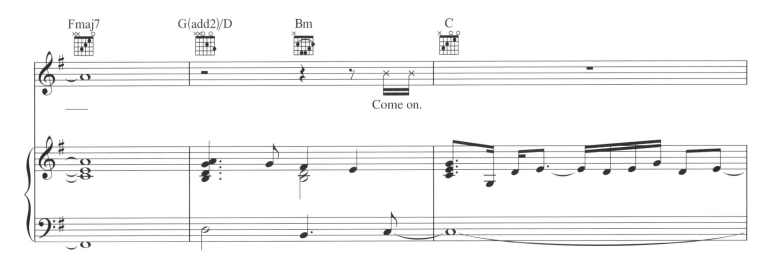

Come on.

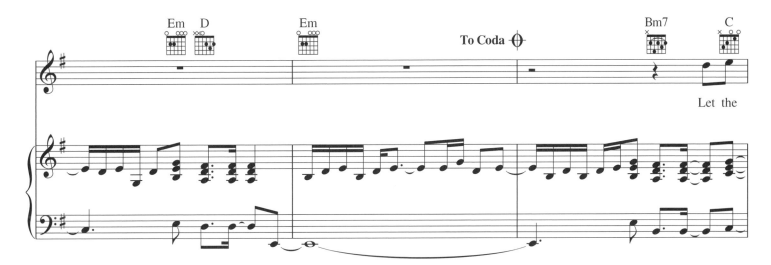

Let the

groove _____ get in-to you.

D.S. al Coda
(take 2nd ending)

Come on, _ now. Are you

CODA

Are you com-f'ta-ble ___ right there, right there. Let the

groove get in ___ there, there, right there. Are you com-f'ta-ble ___ right there, right there. Let the

groove get in ___ there, there, right there. Are you groove get in, ___ there, there, right there.

Are you

com - f'ta - ble? ___   Are you

com - f'ta - ble? ___   Are you

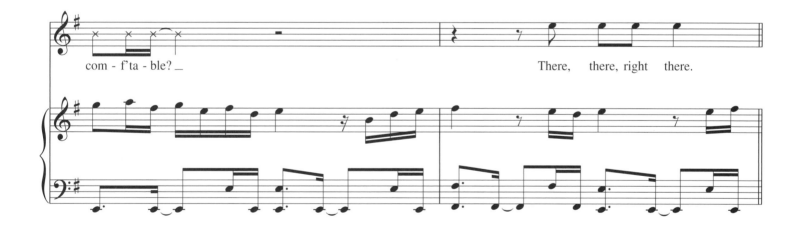

com - f'ta - ble? ___   There,   there, right   there.

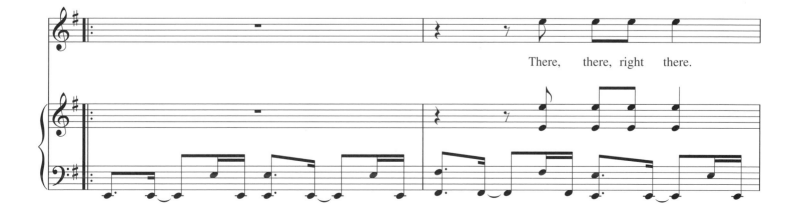

There,   there, right   there.

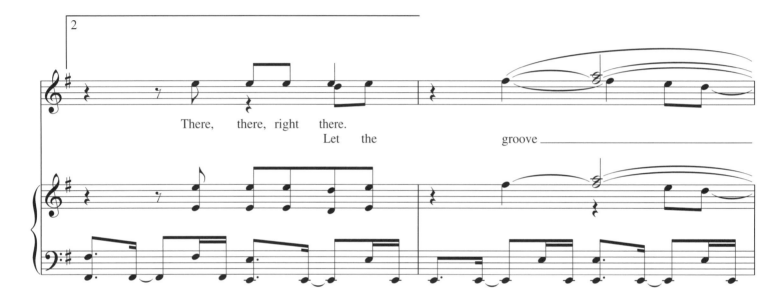

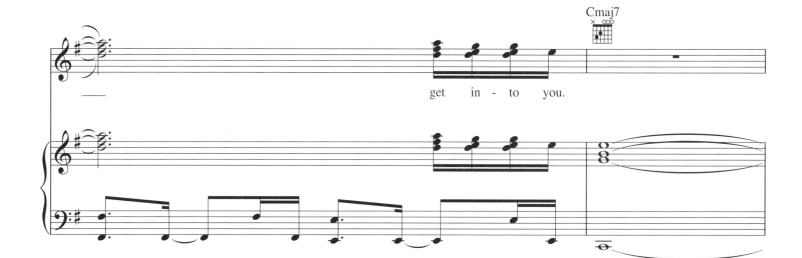

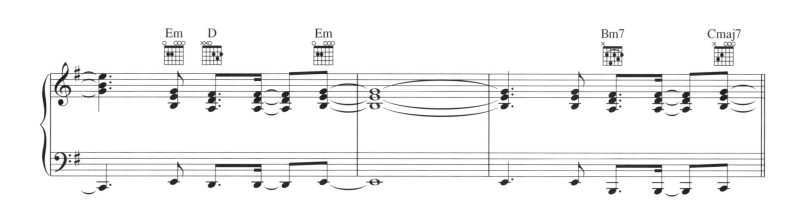

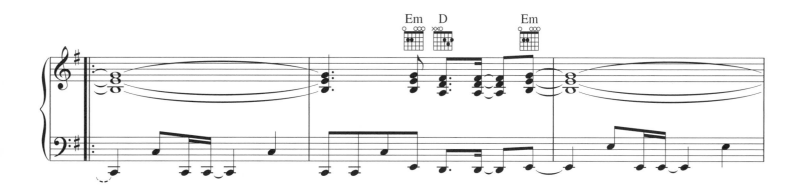

groove get in. All night __ long, _____ you can let the

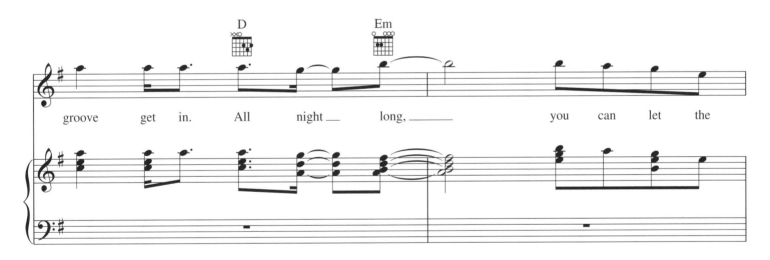

groove get in. All night __ long, _____ just let the

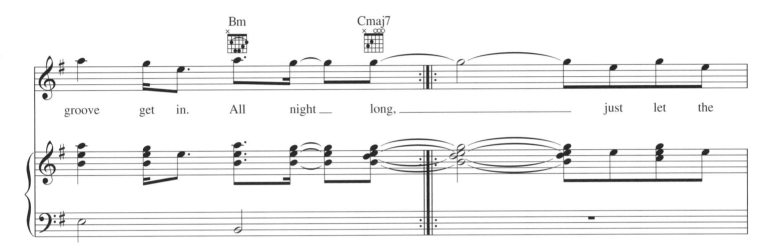

groove get in. All night __ long, _____ you can let the

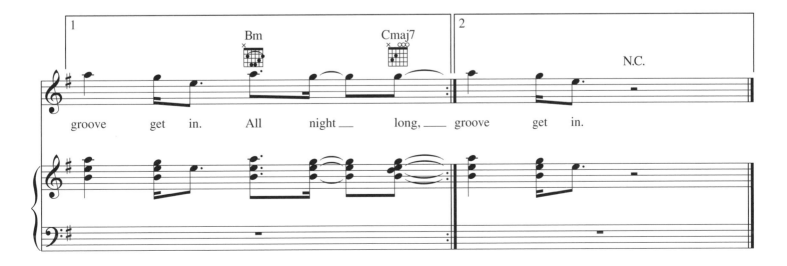

groove get in. All night __ long, __ groove get in.

MIRRORS

Words and Music by JUSTIN TIMBERLAKE,
JAMES FAUNTLEROY, JEROME HARMON,
TIM MOSLEY, CHRIS GODBEY and GARLAND MOSLEY

Half-time groove

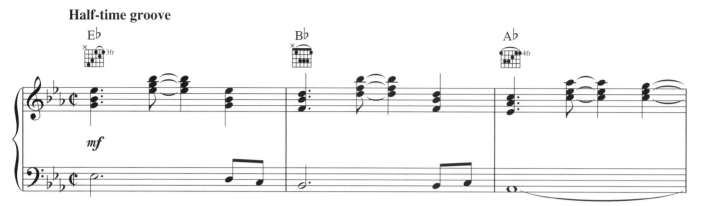

Copyright © 2013 by Universal Music - Z Tunes LLC, Tennman Tunes, Almo Music Corp., Underdog West Songs, Fauntleroy Music,
Warner-Tamerlane Publishing Corp., Jerome Harmon Productions, WB Music Corp., Virginia Beach Music, B Max Entertainment Publishing and 757 Music
All Rights for Tennman Tunes Administered by Universal Music - Z Tunes LLC
All Rights for Underdog West Songs and Fauntleroy Music Controlled and Administered by Almo Music Corp.
All Rights for Jerome Harmon Productions Administered by Warner-Tamerlane Publishing Corp.
All Rights for Virginia Beach Music Administered by WB Music Corp.
International Copyright Secured   All Rights Reserved

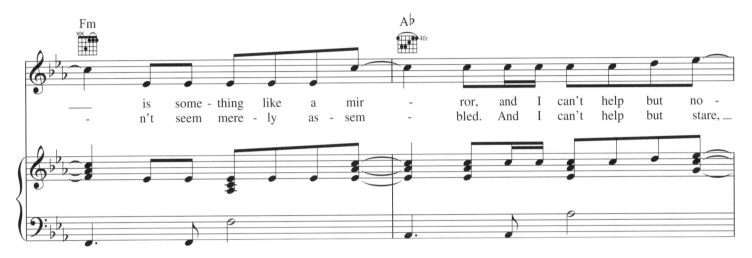

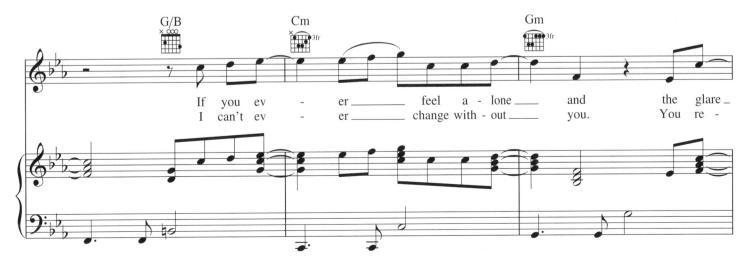

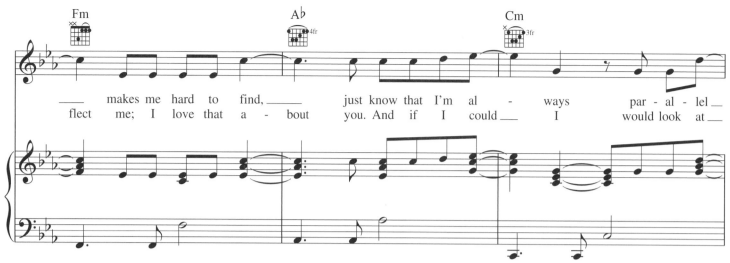

'Cause I don't wan-na lose __ you now. __ I'm look-ing

right at the oth-er half of me. The va-can-cy that sat in my heart __ is a space __ that now you hold. __

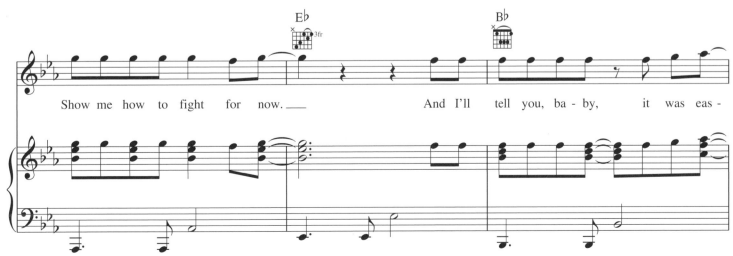

Show me how to fight for now. __ And I'll tell you, ba-by, it was eas-

-y com-ing back here to you once I fig-ured it out. _____ You were right _

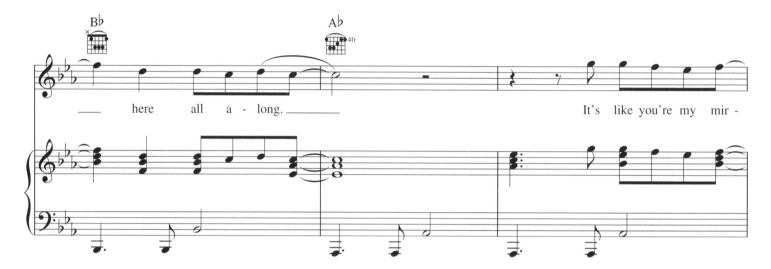

_____ here all a-long. _____ It's like you're my mir-

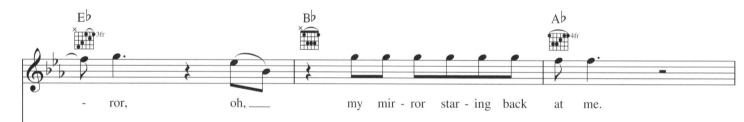

-ror, oh, ___ my mir-ror star-ing back at me.

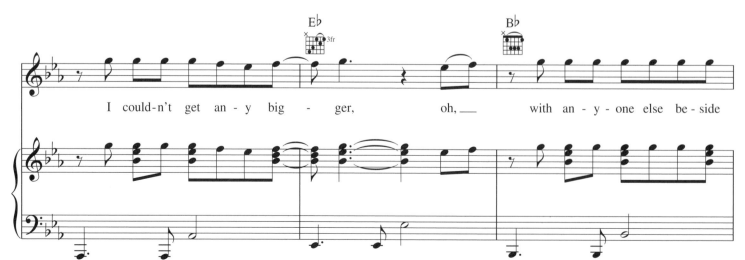

I could-n't get an-y big-ger, oh, ___ with an-y-one else be-side

of me. And now, it's clear as this prom - ise that we're mak -

- ing, two re - flec - tions in - to one.___ 'Cause it's like you're my mir -

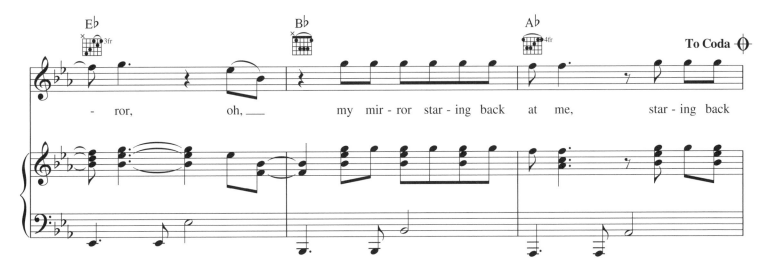

- ror, oh, ___ my mir - ror star - ing back at me, star - ing back

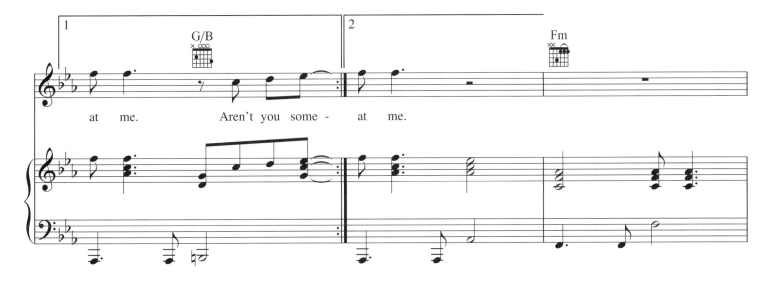

at me. Aren't you some - at me.

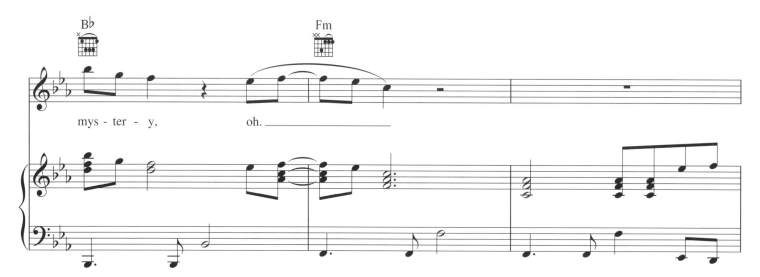

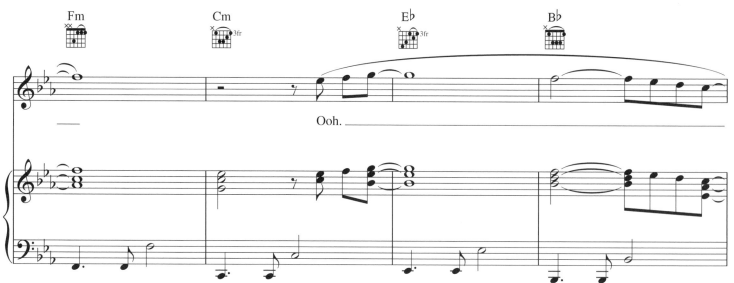

Ooh. _____

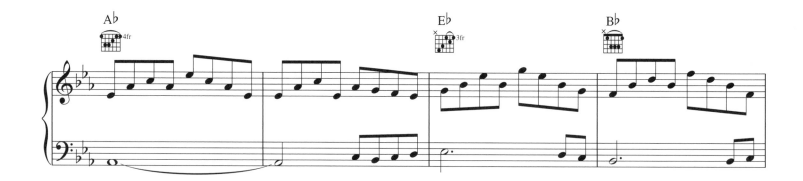

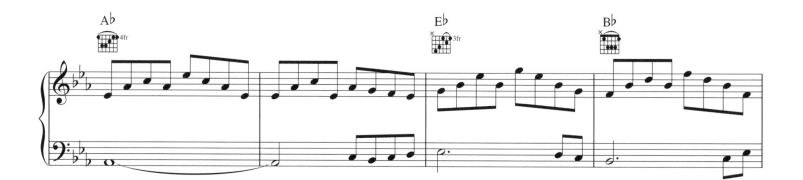

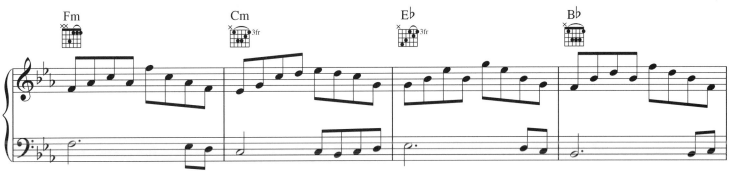

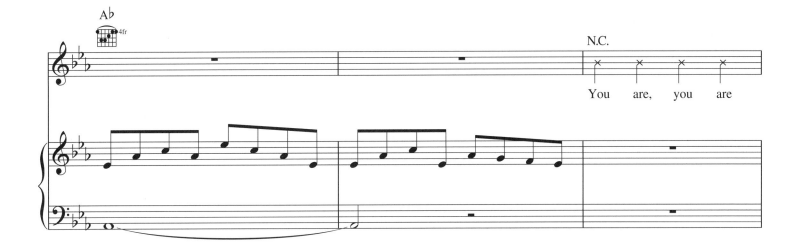

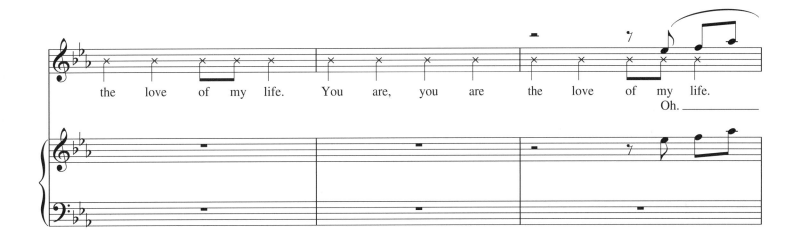

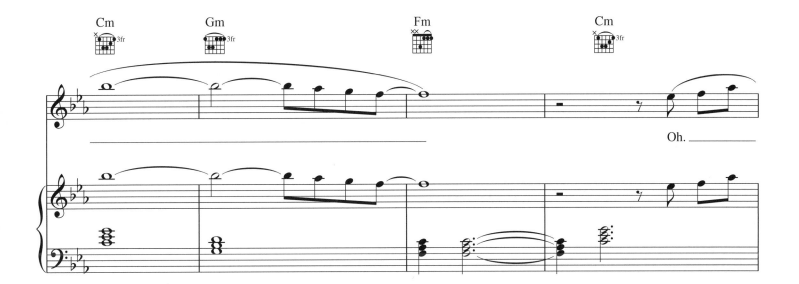

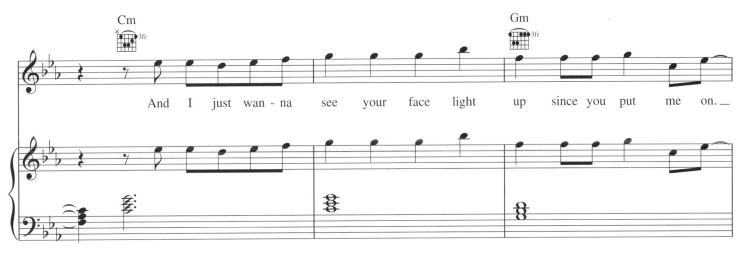

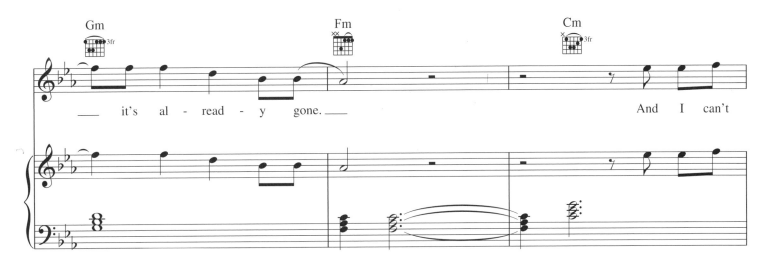

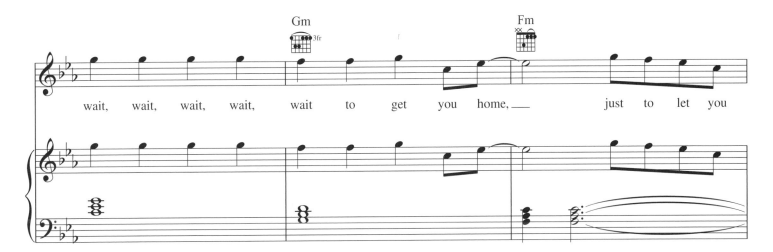

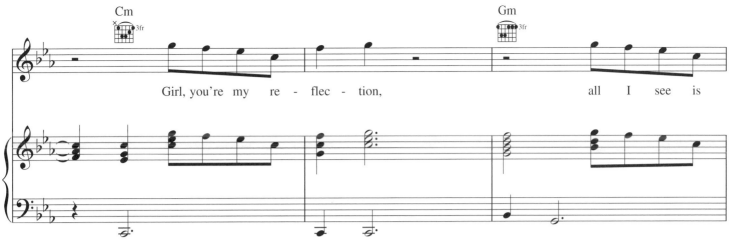

Girl, you're my re - flec - tion, all I see is

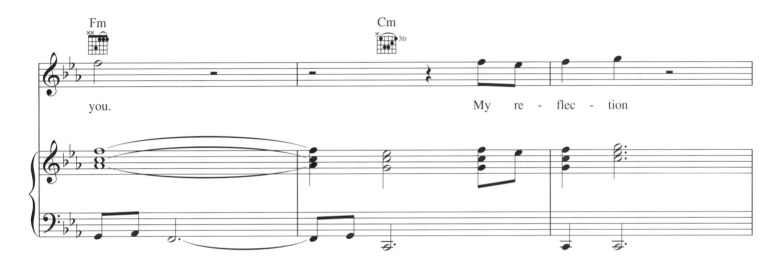

you. My re - flec - tion

in ev - 'ry - thing I do. You're my re -

flec - tion and all I ___ see ___ is you. ___

Ooh.

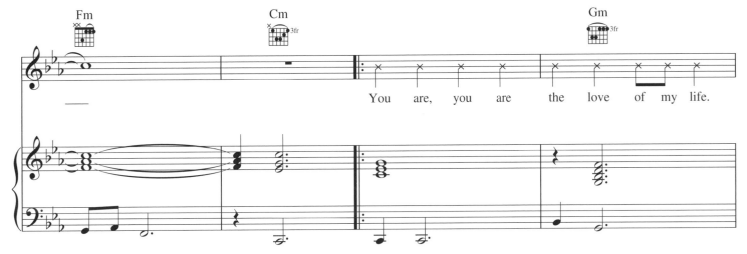

You are, you are the love of my life.

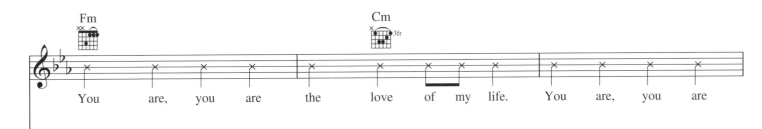

You are, you are the love of my life. You are, you are

the love of my life. You are, you are the love of my life. the love of my life.

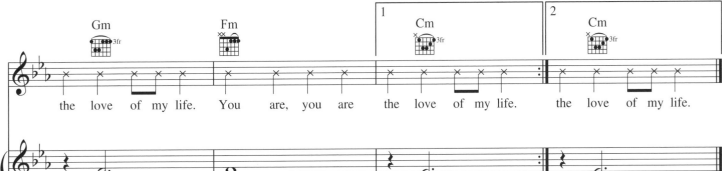

BLUE OCEAN FLOOR

Words and Music by JUSTIN TIMBERLAKE,
JAMES FAUNTLEROY, JEROME HARMON,
TIM MOSLEY and CHRIS GODBEY

Ambient Ballad

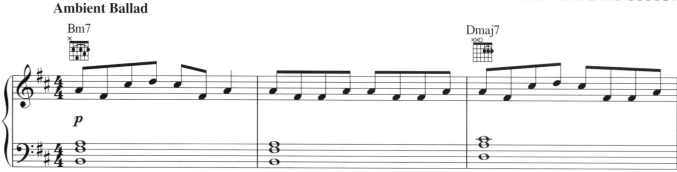

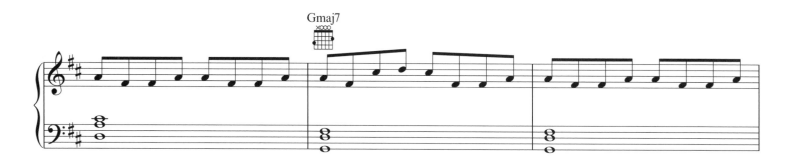

Fre - quen -
Shell made

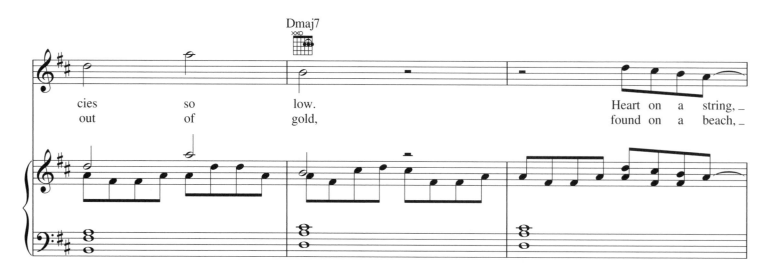

cies so low.
out of gold,

Heart on a string, _
found on a beach, _

Copyright © 2013 by Universal Music - Z Tunes LLC, Tennman Tunes, Almo Music Corp., Underdog West Songs, Fauntleroy Music,
Warner-Tamerlane Publishing Corp., Jerome Harmon Productions, WB Music Corp., Virginia Beach Music and B Max Entertainment Publishing
All Rights for Tennman Tunes Administered by Universal Music - Z Tunes LLC
All Rights for Underdog West Songs and Fauntleroy Music Controlled and Administered by Almo Music Corp.
All Rights for Jerome Harmon Productions Administered by Warner-Tamerlane Publishing Corp.
All Rights for Virginia Beach Music Administered by WB Music Corp.
International Copyright Secured   All Rights Reserved

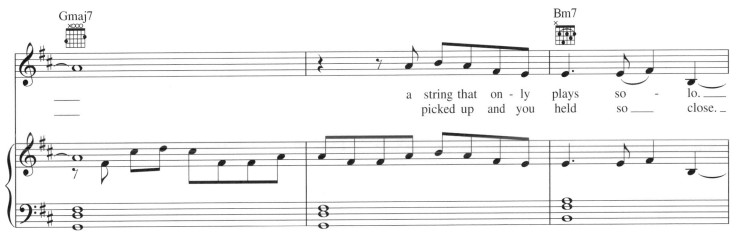

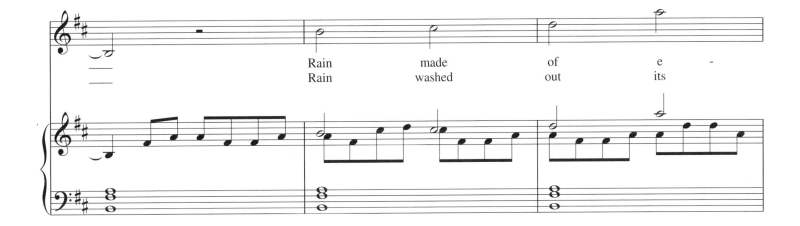

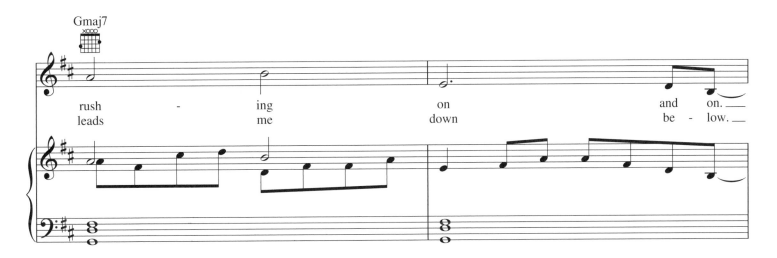

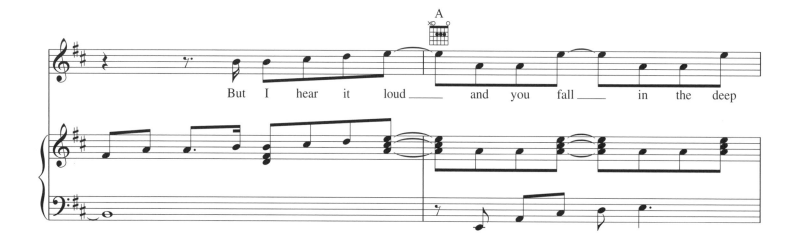

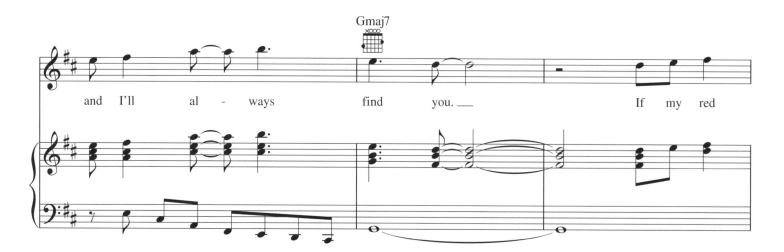

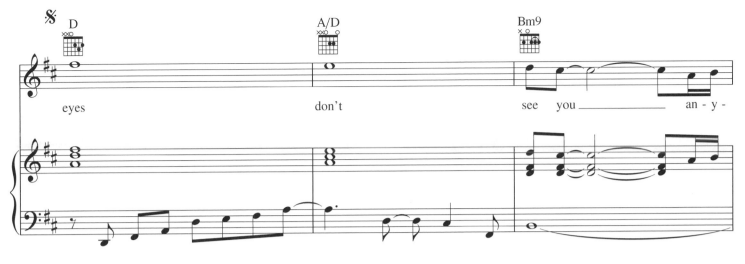

eyes   don't   see you _____ an - y -

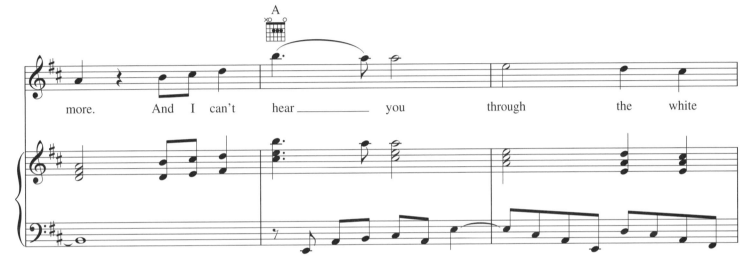

more. And I can't hear _____ you   through   the   white

noise.   Just send your heart - beat, I   go

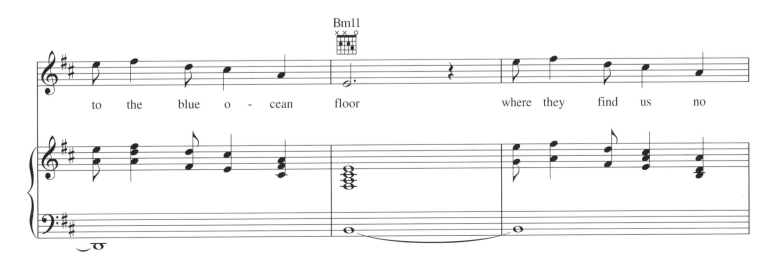

to   the   blue o - cean   floor   where they find us no

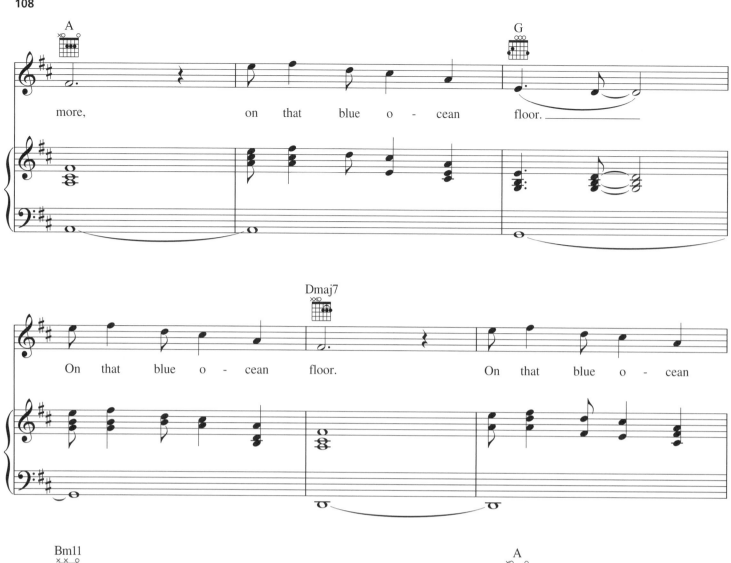

more, on that blue o - cean floor. _____

On that blue o - cean floor. On that blue o - cean

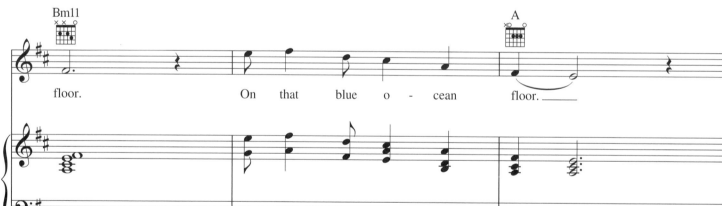

floor. On that blue o - cean floor. _____

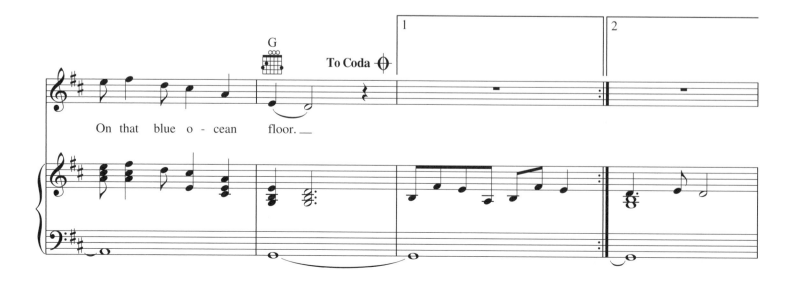

On that blue o - cean floor. _____

Twen-ty thou-sand leagues a - way, catch up to you on the same day.

Trav - el at the speed of light, think-ing the same thought at the same time.

Heart beats at a stead - y pace, I'll let the rhy-thm show me the way.

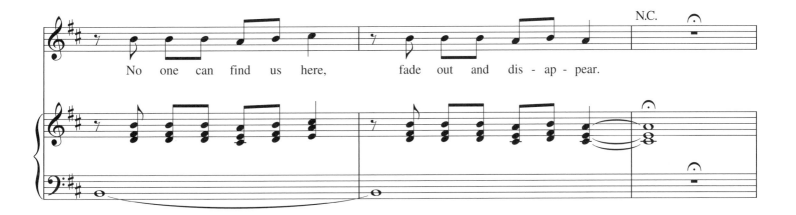

No one can find us here, fade out and dis - ap - pear.

D.S. al Coda

If my red

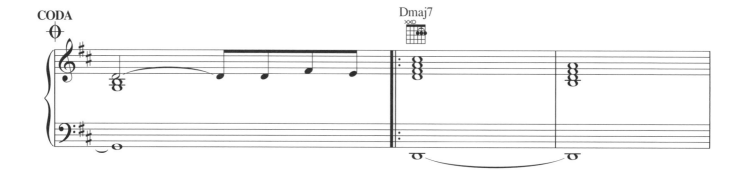

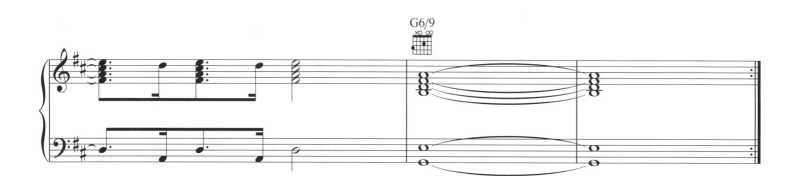